Praise for *I Found Jesus in the Stock Market*

I have had the privilege of working in the financial services world for over forty-five years. Many things come and go, some good some bad. Fifteen to twenty years ago I began to see the development of BRI, and have watched it mature over the last number of years. All new ideas take time to mature as many questions need to be answered as the new idea is taking root. Cassie went through her own evaluation and skepticism and asked most, if not all, of the relevant questions. This book is written by a well- trained and experienced professional as well as a very spiritually- mature woman who has an incredible ability to communicate. This book will answer almost any question that you would have about BRI investing. I highly, highly recommend this book to any serious thinker about using God's resources for God's purposes. It is my privilege to endorse this book.

Ron Blue, Founding Director
Kingdom Advisors,
best-selling author of Master Your Money
www.KingdomAdvisors.com

Cassandra has written a wonderful blend of very practical advice regarding best use of our stewardship of God's resources and His power of redemption and renewal. Her life is an inspiration and also a caution for those still caught in the world's trap of measuring our worth by our accomplishments and performance.

Buck Jacobs, Founder
C12 Group
Author of A Strategic Plan for Ministry
www.c12group.com

I Found Jesus in the Stock Market is one of the most informative and important books on investing that I have ever read. It is a must read for all those who are serious about serving God with all of their resources. Cassandra Laymon is a master at educating on the concepts of Biblically Responsible Investing and presents the material in a manner that is concise and easy to understand. Her passion is contagious and the Biblical foundation that she has woven into the education is extremely powerful. Her personal testimony is so genuine and a true example of how God will bless those who follow His guidance. Both Cassandra and this book are true inspirations and gifts to the market leaders today. After reading this book, I am now one hundred percent committed to making sure that every investment I am involved in meets the criteria of Biblically Responsible Investing.

Mary Messuti
President and CEO,
Christian Business Women's Connection (CBWC)
www.cbwc.biz

I FOUND JESUS IN THE STOCK MARKET
HOW BIBLICALLY RESPONSIBLE INVESTING CAN CHANGE YOUR HEART, TOO

By CASSANDRA LAYMON

Open Door Publications

I Found Jesus in the Stock Market
How Biblically Responsible Investing
Can Change Your Heart, Too
Copyright © 2016 by Cassandra Laymon
ISBN: 978-0-9960985-7-1

Scripture quotations are taken from the Holy Bible, New Living Translation, copyright © 1996, 2004, 2007. Used by permission of Tyndale House Publishers Inc., Carol Stream, Illinois 60188. All rights reserved.

The purpose of this book is to educate and entertain. The author and/or publisher do not guarantee that anyone following these techniques, suggestions, tips, ideas, or strategies will become successful. The author and/or publisher shall have neither liability nor responsibility to anyone with respect to any loss or damage caused, or alleged to be caused, directly or indirectly by the information contained in this book. The information presented in this book is for education and/or general information only. It does not consider your personal investment objectives or financial situation and does not make personalized recommendations. It is not intended to provide specific legal, investing, accounting, tax, or other professional advice. Individuals should consult with the appropriate professional to help answer questions about their specific situations or needs prior to taking any action based on this information.

Cover Design by Genevieve Cosdon, Lavodesign.com
Published by
Open Door Publications
2113 Stackhouse Dr.
Yardley, PA 19067
www.OpenDoorPublications.com

Dedication

For my husband Rick.
Thank you for serving as my guide
on this amazing journey.
I am blessed beyond measure.

Table of Contents

Foreword

When Cassie asked me to write the Foreword for her second book, I was both surprised and delighted. Surprised because I have never written a Foreword before and few people outside of our Kingdom Advisors circle really know who I am. Delighted because I am her husband, biggest fan and to some extent, a guide on this journey.

From the moment we first met in Chicago at a financial planning conference in 2010, I knew there was something very special about Cassie. We became fast friends, first professionally and over time on a more personal level. When we started dating long distance some eighteen months later, I distinctly remember her kiddingly recounting her assessment of our first meeting: "Too bad he is so churchy!" Interesting how God works.

We had only been dating a few short months and we both knew that God was calling us into marriage. As a fun bonding exercise in our budding relationship, Cassie suggested we write Thanksgiving letters to each other looking back as if we were eighty-five years old (She too is something of a Visioneer!) Among other things I wrote to her in my letter, I mentioned what an amazing woman of God she had grown to be over our many years together. Little did I know how the seeds of faith sown in her childhood would quickly blossom into the guiding force of her life. She has grown and followed after our Lord's calling in such marvelous ways I could not then imagine. From being full of hard questions and doubts to becoming a faithful Christ follower and one of the significant leaders of the Biblically Responsible Investing movements today, I could not be more proud of her!

As for the book, it is a very sensible exposition of the "whys" and "how to's" of implementing Biblically Responsible Investing principles bookended by Cassie's personal and quite vulnerable testimony—from where she was spiritually at the start of her investigation of BRI, to how the journey transformed her life as she encountered the truth of God's living Word, to His instruction for us along the way. In like fashion, *I Found Jesus in the Stock Market* is a book about the kinetic power BRI has to change the culture and business practices of corporate America, but far more importantly (and this is the real message), how it can transform the hearts of individual investors and advisors just as it has with Cassie. Open yours and join us on the ride!

Rick Laymon
CEO, Beacon Wealth Consultants

Introduction

Does God really care how you invest your money?

If He were to take a look at your portfolio right now—the companies that you profit from, and the business practices of those companies—would He approve?

Could you be investing in companies that fund the abortion industry, or pornography, or promote addictions or anti-family values—without even knowing it?

These were the questions I faced when introduced to the concept of Biblically Responsible Investing (BRI). I had never heard of it, I didn't understand it, and honestly, I wasn't sure it would or could make a difference in my life.

I had been away from the church for over two decades, but my new boyfriend (and potential fiancée) was an all-in Christ follower, so I was faced with the challenge of learning as much as I could about God's Word and the ultimate stewardship question: "What would Jesus have me do with the possessions and blessings I've been given?"

Whether you are mature in your faith or new to the truths of Biblical teaching, you may be shocked to learn that a significant portion of your investment portfolio is likely invested in businesses with practices that oppose your faith—even if your financial advisor is a Christian.

You probably make charitable donations to fund ministries that support your beliefs, and at the same time, you are profiting from practices that go against those same values.

As a community of Christians, we are faced with an opportunity to align our faith values with our investments through Biblically Responsible Investing. In the chapters ahead you will learn:

- Where investing fits into the bigger picture of stewardship
- How to define Biblically Responsible Investing
- The case I was able to build for BRI that convinced me this is the only way for Christians to invest
- What the Bible says about investing and profits
- Answers to the objections advisors and investors have about BRI
- How you, too, can learn what business practices you are invested in
- How the world would be different if we, as Christians, all invested this way
- An action plan for next steps

Biblically Responsible Investing literally changed my life and brought me back to the church as a committed Believer. I hope my story inspires you.

Part I
Laying the Groundwork

Chapter 1
The Quest

Have you ever found yourself daydreaming about the life you were *supposed* to have? Looking forward to that day in the future when everything has been checked off your list and you can stop running so hard? Wanting more and more, but no matter how much you have, it will never be enough?

If I had to choose a theme for the first forty years of my life, it would either be "more is always better" or "good is never good enough." From a very early age, I was constantly striving for approval and never finding contentment in my life. I had a number of achievements under my belt, but it was never enough and I wanted more, and more, and more.

In school I got straight A's and made the honor roll. That wasn't enough. I played the piano, played saxophone in concert band, jazz, and marching band, sang in the chorus, and was the accompanist for the pop chorus. That wasn't enough. I was on the swim team, played softball, and was on the men's golf team. I earned twelve varsity letters. That wasn't enough. When I was a senior, I won the countywide young women's pageant, and went on to compete at the state level. Never, ever, did it feel like enough. I could not slow down and enjoy the present moment, not even for one minute.

In college I dropped many of the extracurricular activities in exchange for more time for studies. I majored in physical therapy, which was a relatively intense program compared to the lighter majors of my roommates. I also became a resident assistant in my dorm, which really was a full-time job.

At that time, my constant striving and underlying anxiety took a different direction. I developed an eating disorder, which was really a way to try to exercise some control over my life. I got caught up in the college drinking scene, which was especially dangerous as my dad was an alcoholic. I glimpsed the future of my life on that same path. I started a pattern of dating the wrong men. I had a habit of picking men who were not serious about a relationship—or much of anything else. I was attracted to their entertaining personalities, but when it came to anything serious, like holding down a job, they were not interested. I always felt as if I had to be the responsible one in the relationship if anything productive was going to get done.

Little did I realize at the time, I was trying to fill a

"God-sized" hole in my heart.

I was brought up in the church, a good Presbyterian girl. My mom was, and remains, a pillar in the church, one of those people you can count on for anything that is needed at any time. She made sure my brother and I were at church every Sunday, and I enjoyed participating in choir and youth group. But one Sunday in my senior year of high school, my Sunday School teacher made a comment that "If God wasn't real, we would make him up," meaning that we, as a culture would create a God to worship if he didn't exist. He was a Believer, but that offhanded comment planted a seed of doubt, and by the time I reached college I had completely abandoned my faith.

As soon as I graduated and started working as a physical therapist, I was back at the game of over-commitment, constantly running, but toward an unknown target. I had this vision of what my life would be like—someday. I got married soon out of college to fulfill the first check on my to-do list, "Married." I thought being married would fill me up. That ended in disaster only one year later. Two years after my divorce, I married once again, to a very nice man. We did not share the same values or aspirations, and again, I found myself in an unfulfilling relationship. I believed that two marriages were enough for anyone, so I made a conscious decision to stick it out and make my marriage work. I decided to put my focus on my career. I had a vision that I would be doing great things someday; I just didn't know what those "great things" were. In the meantime, I was willing to do whatever it took to get ahead. Besides putting in extra time on nights and weekends for work, I pursued a master's degree in adult education. School was a perfect distraction from my marriage, and it gave me many opportunities at work to do presentations and teach, which I loved. Being in graduate school flamed my passion for learning, which has continued to this day.

Once I had my master's degree, I was promoted to run the Organizational Development department for the hospital system where I was working, where we employed 5,000 employees in six locations. My boss was even more of an overachiever than I was, and made my urgency-filled, overcommitted life look as if I was standing still. The demands on my time were tremendous, and, quite frankly, unrealistic. I saw very little of my husband or young son. There was one week when I was home for ten total hours for the entire week. I came home, slept for an hour, showered, and went back to work. It's difficult to recover from that level of exhaustion, but that was the pace that I was trying to keep.

As you can imagine, my schedule was not conducive to a healthy marriage. But I kept pushing on, sure that "someday" I would have that dream life: enough money, enough time, enough love, so I would be able to relax and enjoy myself. I became increasingly disappointed in my marriage, convinced that if my husband had as much drive as I did, I wouldn't have to work so hard.

At this point, my boss encouraged me to go and get my MBA. I am a disciple of the "short-term pain, long-term gain" school of thought, so I decided that while I was working full time, I would also attend grad school full time, taking fifteen credits each semester. That would allow me to finish in twenty-four months.

You can imagine the level of craziness that goes into that kind of schedule. I obviously missed much of my son's kindergarten and first grade years, including his kindergarten graduation. It will come as no surprise that this season of fully committing myself to work and school also marked the end of my second marriage.

Once I had finished my MBA, I did not take time to mourn the loss of my marriage. I realized that there was an even BIGGER and BETTER world out there for me. Without a second thought (because, really, I was only thinking about me) I quit my secure and well-paying job, moved in with a new boyfriend, and started my career as a financial advisor with a major Wall Street firm.

I quickly realized that, along with many of the new recruits who started with me, I had not been taught the skills needed to best serve my clients. It was all about getting the sale. I was taught that it really didn't matter what was *best* for the client, as long as I actually did not cause harm. I was never comfortable with that approach, and took my job of managing other people's money very seriously. I felt an immense responsibility to do the right thing, and spent endless hours reading, studying, and taking continuing education courses on my own so that I could help these people who had put their trust in me.

The managers who hired me were honest about the pressure of the job. When I was hired, they told me that only five percent of new advisors actually "make it" in the business. Therefore, they predicted of the thousand advisors they had hired that year, only fifty would succeed in the business. They overestimated.

However, I assured them that *I* would be one of the fifty who made it, because I was the queen of hard work.

This new career placed an unprecedented level of stress on me. I needed to provide for my son, and I now had the added pressure of hitting sales targets that could not be missed. This also opened up new opportunities for "schmoozing" with clients, which meant lots of drinking and late nights, which only served to fuel my sense of emptiness.

I was trying in every way I knew to fill the void in my life. God never occurred to me as the answer. While I had felt very comfortable in my small town church growing up, for me church was more about community than it was about Christ. What I most enjoyed was socializing with my friends and their families each Sunday. As I grew older I started to see Christians as rigid and judgmental, often condemning others when their own house was not in order. In fairness, my exposure to Christians was limited, and I didn't take the time to find a loving and accepting church once I left home.

A few short months after I started my new job as a financial advisor, one of the hospitals from the health system where I had previously worked was scheduled to close. The news came out in April. It was a heart-wrenching time for the employees and the community. Not knowing exactly how to roll out a financial education program of that magnitude, the Human Resources department contacted me and asked me to assist them in guiding a significant number of employees with making decisions about their pension and retirement money. This was an amazing opportunity for me and an unbelievable blessing to help me to launch my new career.

In an effort to help as many people as possible, I moved back into my old office at the hospital and met with employees at their convenience. For the third shift workers, that sometimes meant meeting at three o'clock in the morning. They were, of course, very grateful to have help since there are not many crazy advisors willing to meet in the middle of the night! I was exhausted, but determined to help them, as well as to meet my sales target that was coming up at the end of July. According to my perfect plan and calculations, if the hospital closed on schedule in June, the employees' retirement money would rollover to me in July. That's how it was supposed to happen. If only I was in charge.

Due to a number of delays, the hospital did not close in June. Or July. During my July evaluation, not only was I not a top producer in my class, I was in the lowest level of production. I'm lucky I didn't get fired. Finally, on August 16th, the hospital closed. This meant the retirement funds would reach me in October.

You may recall the stock market crash of 2008 happened in September. The retirement funds that were moving to me had all been in sitting in cash, so they were not exposed to the same devastating losses that most of the country experienced. In October, the market reached the lowest point since the tech bubble burst nearly a decade before.

I was extraordinarily grateful that my clients had been spared any kind of loss in this meltdown. That month I met with clients, processed paperwork, and closed a lot of business. Around November, when the bulk of the work was done, I was finally able to step back and look at what had happened in an objective way.

It was, in my mind, a miracle. If everything had gone according to *my* plan, all of my clients, who were now out of a job with no real prospects in sight, would have lost fifty percent of their retirement savings virtually overnight. Certainly, my career would have been over even before it had begun, and that would have been devastating to me. But so much worse, each of my clients would have experienced an earth-shattering financial setback, which would have been hard for me to live with even though it would not have been my fault (the market is clearly out of my control).

Instead, due to this divine delay, I was able to help my clients to grow their wealth during a time that was difficult for so many. As I reflected back over that year, I was able to see God's hand in my life.

Around that time, I had started to make some new friends who were more spiritually inclined. They would ask about my spiritual life and encourage me to pray. I should be clear that while these friends believed in God, it was more of an "anything goes" approach to faith. I still rejected a formal church because I perceived it to be judgmental and legalistic. These friends opened my mind up to the idea of God and how much I needed Him in my life. I started a regular prayer and meditation practice, and was able to see how God had been writing a story over my life that was so much better than what I had been able to see for myself.

About a year later, I determined a big firm was not the right place for me to grow my business. I was most concerned about doing the right thing for my clients, and my employer was most concerned about charging the highest fees. I decided to become an independent advisor so I could serve my client's best interests and cater to the healthcare workers who I felt so called to serve. I even wrote a retirement book for nurses (*The Retirement Game for Nurses: 9 Simple and Sensible Strategies,* which is published under my maiden name, Cassandra Chandler) and spoke at hospitals and nursing events about making good financial decisions.

During the five years I was building my fledgling business, my relationship with my boyfriend became progressively worse. I had allowed myself to become his glorified personal assistant and nanny. I spent all of my free time running kids to their activities and checking items off my boyfriend's very long to-do list. If I didn't drop everything and come running, I was berated for being a very selfish person.

He had become very controlling and emotionally abusive. My reaction was to become angry, resentful, and depressed. I literally could not stand myself. I had made yet another bad relationship decision and felt trapped. This was my rock bottom. I was very tired of these failed relationships, and I desperately wanted to make this one work. At the same time, I started asking myself, "at what expense?"

With the encouragement of some wise friends, I went home one day to announce the moving trucks were on the way. Two days later I found myself living in a brand-new town with no friends or family. While on some level I looked at this as one more failed relationship, I knew I had escaped a particularly bad situation. One night as I was crying myself to sleep, I decided that I would go to church that Sunday to thank God for delivering me from that relationship. As I look back, I have to chuckle; how generous of me to make a deal with God to go to church one Sunday to thank him for my blessings!

That Sunday marked a turning point in my life. I still remember the title of the sermon that my pastor gave that day at church: "New Beginnings." I knew I was right where God wanted me to be. I found that I loved my new church, and started to attend regularly and get more involved with church activities. It was a wonderful community of Believers, and I was welcomed with open arms.

I had only been back at church as a "regular" for a few short months when I started dating a financial advisor, Rick, who would later become my husband. When we first started dating, he invited me to a company retreat with his team and their spouses. Being with these couples was different than anything I had ever experienced. I was used to being around unhappy couples who spent as little time together as possible. On this retreat, I observed couples who loved and respected each other, and weren't afraid to say or show it. It was overwhelming to me, and I knew that this was the kind of relationship I wanted in my life.

When I first met Rick, a year earlier at a conference in Chicago, he told me that for the last fifteen years he had been practicing something called Biblically Responsible Investing or BRI, which is defined as investing in a way that seeks to please and glorify God as a vital act of worship. As a financial advisor, I was intrigued but I have to be honest: I had never heard of Biblically Responsible Investing, and I really had no clue what it was. I was concerned that if we decided to get married, I would have to completely rethink my approach to money. All my life I was taught never to mix business with politics or religion, and I had been trained to manage money in a way that completely left God out of the equation.

I had a big decision to make: Would I keep my business separate from Rick's? If we merged our businesses it would mean that I, too, would have to invest with this Biblical approach to money. Being a very smart man, Rick made no demands on me. He felt very strongly that this is how God calls us to invest our money, but he challenged me to find out for myself. I decided to put on my investigative reporter hat, and I spent one full year on a quest to learn about what God says about how we invest our (really His!) money. While I did want to marry Rick, I was not willing to blindly implement Biblical Investing before I understood and agreed with it.

As the wise King Solomon once said:

Wisdom is always distant and difficult to find. I searched everywhere, determined to find wisdom and to understand the reason for things. I was determined to prove to myself that wickedness is stupid and that foolishness is madness.

Ecclesiastes 7:24-25 (NLT)

I decided that when there were ideas or information I didn't understand I would investigate and work to comprehend the meaning and purpose behind the words in Scripture. I thought I was familiar with the Bible because of all those years of Sunday School. What I realized was that I was pretty well acquainted with Genesis, and the Christmas and Easter stories. For the first time in my life I was determined to read the Bible and see how it applied to my life.

At the same time I started reading the Bible, I read Lee Strobel's *The Case for Christ*, and that helped accelerate my learning about Jesus. I loved the factual approach of the book; it made me want to learn more about Jesus and his ministry here on Earth.

I was really searching for the truth.

Over the next few chapters I will share what I learned over that year. I will tell you up front that it is not my goal to bring a unique perspective to Biblically Responsible Investing. I am going to share the information I studied and learned from the pioneers and thought leaders in the Biblically Responsible Investing movement, all in my own words, just as if we were sitting down over a cup of coffee one afternoon.

I hope you will not only read my personal "Case for Biblically Responsible Investing," but that you will stay to the end to hear how this journey literally transformed my life.

Don't copy the behavior and customs of this world, but let God transform you into a new person by changing the way you think. Then you will learn to know God's will for you, which is good and pleasing and perfect.

Romans 12:2 (NLT)

Chapter 2

Does God Really Care How You Invest Your Money?

Seek the kingdom of God above all else, and live righteously, and he will give you everything you need.
Matthew 6:33 (NLT)

I think it is important to kick this chapter off with a topic that you already know something about: stewardship. I don't know about you, but when I used to hear the word "stewardship" I thought of the guys that pass out pledge cards and envelopes each November at church. That stewardship was a once a year activity, synonymous with giving. The more I have studied the Biblical principles of money, the more I realize how all-encompassing the concept of stewardship is.

Stewardship is about using your time, talents, and treasure to the best of your ability to maximize your impact and blessing in this world. During our time together, I hope to convince you that you also have the ability to be a good steward with your *influence*. When you learn important concepts that can bless the people in your circle of influence, you have a great opportunity to make a difference in their lives.

If you ask the question, "What would Jesus want me to do with all of my possessions and blessings?" you will understand the essence of stewardship.

In this book we are going to focus on the "treasure" or the financial piece of the stewardship pie.

Let's start by looking at a chart on Financial Stewardship. This chart encompasses all the parts of your financial life:

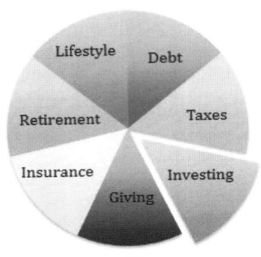

- Lifestyle
- Taxes
- Debt
- Giving
- Retirement
- Insurance
- And, of course, Investing, which is what we are going to focus on for this discussion

There are two fundamental truths that are important for framing our stewardship discussion. I believe, as Christians, we are all on board with these truths, but let's start together at the beginning.

Truth 1: God owns everything[1]

The earth is the Lord's, and everything in it. The world and all its people belong to him.

Psalm 24:1 (NLT)

I think this is something on which we can all agree. We know this to be true in theory, but how often do we really live our lives this way? I think most of us think of

---

[1] E.G. "Jay" Link, "Does God Care How We Invest?" Life Stewardship Newsletter, page 1, paragraph 2, http://www.legacywealthwisdom.com/pdfs/Does%20God%20Care%20How%20We%20Invest.pdf

our tithe, the ten percent of our income that we donate to church, as belonging to God. But what about the other ninety percent? Doesn't that *also* belong to God? How would our financial decisions change if we always kept that in mind? Would it influence our decisions?

I am reminded of the story of R.G. LeTourneau, a Christian inventor, businessman, and entrepreneur best known for inventing earthmoving machinery and road construction equipment that revolutionized his industry. Early on, R.G. found himself in debt. Fortunately, he had decided the Lord was his business partner, and he would let God solve all his business problems. R.G. was always faithful, and over the course of his lifetime, he not only paid off those debts, but became highly successful, and went on to become a multimillionaire in the first half of the twentieth century.

This is my favorite part of his story: In 1935, recognizing the unprecedented success of their company, R.G.'s wife, Evelyn, suggested they change their financial "split" with God. They became famous for the "reverse tithe"—living on ten percent of their income and giving ninety percent for the spread of the Gospel. By 1959, after giving $10 million in donations to religious and educational works, the LeTourneau Foundation was still worth some $40 million. [2]

Now, there is a man who knew that God owns

---

[2] "RG LeTourneau – Earthmoving Innovator," Giants for God, http://www.giantsforgod.com/rg-letourneau/

everything!

Truth 2: It's our job to carefully and wisely manage *everything* God entrusts to us according to His wishes.[3]

And if you are untrustworthy about worldly wealth, who will trust you with the true riches of heaven?

Luke 16:11 (NLT)

To tie these two truths together, it only makes sense to assume that we should invest God's money in a way that would please and honor him.

- Would you make different financial decisions if you followed this maxim? What would change in your lifestyle and spending?
- How much debt would you carry?
- What would your monthly savings look like?
- And, of course, the big question: What kind of companies would you invest in? That is a question that I had never considered until I started this journey.

Wherever your treasure is, there the desires of your heart will also be.

Mathew 6:21 (NLT)

---

[3] E.G. "Jay" Link, op. cit. page 20

25

There is a familiar saying, "Show me your checkbook and your calendar, and I will tell you what's important to you." To me that says that whatever we treasure the most controls us, whether we want to admit it or not.

What is Biblically Responsible Investing?

Simply put, Biblically Responsible Investing is a unique approach to investing that seeks to glorify God as an act of worship and to promote Biblical values such as the sanctity of life, family, marriage, etc. Other names for this type of investing are **Faith-Based Investing** and **Morally Responsible Investing**. There are two main components of Biblically Responsible Investing:

Positive Screening

There are many companies seeking to be a blessing in this world, through the products and services they offer, through the way they serve their customers and their employees, and through funding worthy charities and missions. While not publically traded, Chik-fil-A and Hobby Lobby are two well-known examples of the type of companies positive screening seeks to identify.

Negative Screening

On the flip side, there are certain companies that you may choose not to invest in or profit from because their business practices go against God's Word. Here are some examples of business practices that are often screened out of BRI portfolios:

- Abortion: This is obvious. We want to protect life at all stages, and respect God's commandment, "you shall not kill."
- Pornography and Adult Entertainment: I think we can agree that God detests sexual immorality, prostitution, and the seduction that accompanies it. We will talk about that more in Chapter 5.
- Alcohol, Tobacco, and Gambling: If you are not a smoker or an alcoholic, you may think these issues are of no consequence to you. You might be surprised to learn how these companies do everything in their power to create addicts at the youngest age possible, and then profit from their addictions. These are sometimes referred to as "sin stocks," a term used to "identify a stock of a company either directly involved in or associated with activities widely considered to be *unethical or immoral*. Sin stocks are found in sectors whose activities are frowned upon by some or most of society, because they are perceived as *making money from exploiting human weaknesses and frailties*. Sin stock sectors include alcohol, tobacco, gambling, sex-related industries, weapons manufacturers, and the military. Also known as 'sinful stocks,' they are

the polar opposite of ethical investing and Socially Responsible Investing, whose proponents emphasize investments that benefit society." [4]

- Corporate governance: This looks at how a company balances its responsibility to its many stakeholders. Biblical Responsible Investing screening would seek to eliminate companies that price gouge, that employ unfair labor standards, or that overcompensate their executives.

As Believers, we are faced with a real dilemma when it comes to investing: Should I be focused on making the most money, or should I be concerned about the moral nature of those investments? This short introduction may have you wondering what kind of companies you are currently invested in through your retirement and investment accounts. That is an excellent question, which we will answer soon! The question you need to consider at this point is: Does God really care how I invest my money?

---

[4] Weinhold, Tim, "The Smoking Gun of Mutual Funds," Eventide Funds, http://eventidefunds.com/faith-and-business/the-smoking-gun-of-mutual-funds/

The decision to invest in one place rather than another, in one productive sector than another, is always a moral and cultural choice.

Pope John Paul II

PART II
The Case
for Biblically Responsible Investing

I am honored to have an opportunity to share with you what I have learned about Biblical financial principles and Biblically Responsible Investing. There are several thought leaders mentioned in this section who I learned from along the way, through their books, websites, and personal conversations. They have all agreed to let me share their wisdom with you in these next chapters, and I am forever grateful: Ron Blue, Finny Kuruvilla, Dan Hardt, Rusty Leonard, Dwight Short, and my husband, Rick Laymon.

Chapter 3
BRI Bootcamp

When I first met my husband, Rick, and learned that he practiced Biblically Responsible Investing, I was skeptical. It seemed to me to be a bit of a sales gimmick. I had seen so many advertisements and programs promoting the prosperity gospel, and it appeared to be just one more way that religion could be used to pass down guilt and judgment to susceptible churchgoers.

Early on, I asked Rick many questions about BRI. To be honest, they were not the questions of an investigative reporter. They were attacking and challenging questions, set out to put him on the defense. I wanted a debate. I wanted unequivocal answers.

Instead of taking the bait, Rick appreciated I was asking questions, and was unwavering in his faith. Instead of engaging with me in these debates, he lovingly directed me to a number of resources that would help me to get my questions answered.

Several times he mentioned to me I should enroll in

the Kingdom Advisors Core Curriculum training program. Founded by Ron Blue and Larry Burkett, here is the Kingdom Advisors Vision statement:

A Wise Financial Standard. Kingdom Advisors provides advocacy, training, and community for financial professionals who are specialists in offering biblically wise advice. We also offer distinction to our advisors by granting the Qualified Kingdom Advisor™ designation. We are committed to serving advisors along their unique journeys of faith/work integration.[5]

One of my top five strengths on the Strengths Finders test is "Learner." I'm a voracious reader, and take every opportunity to take classes and learn as much as I can on a variety of subjects. I will admit that I was reluctant to start the Kingdom Advisors training for two reasons.

First, I had just finished my CERTIFIED FINANICAL PLANNER™ training and exams, and I was exhausted from the intensity of it. Second, I knew this training would challenge me in ways that stirred up a lot of fear in me.

For most of my life, I didn't really stand firm for much of anything. I was neutral on almost every topic, especially those concerning religion and politics. Most

---

[5] Kingdom Advisors website, https://kingdomadvisors.com/about/vision

of us are trained that this is a good business practice, and that we should never discuss these topics. I couldn't imagine talking to clients about my faith, or theirs. I knew deep down that if I came to believe what was laid out in this program I would have to change the way I did business. I did not feel prepared to do that. I was certain I would lose all my clients, because they would think I had gone crazy and become a kooky Christian.

I want to share some of the basic lessons I learned from Kingdom Advisors that set the foundation for my quest to learn about Biblically Responsible Investing and God's plan for my life. You can find out more about Kingdom Advisors by going to http://www.kingdomadvisors.com.

Knowing to Believing to Doing

"Many Christians believe in Jesus, but fail to think like Jesus."

Ron Blue, Founder of Kingdom Advisors

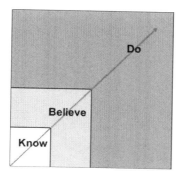

From Kingdom Advisors Core Training Overview, session 2, page 1.

One of the first lessons I learned outlined the process for developing a Biblical philosophy for giving advice. Kingdom Advisors calls this "Knowing to Believing to Doing."[6] When I worked in Organizational Development we called it "Words become Beliefs become Actions." I think this is important to share, because these are the same steps you will have to go through if you decide you will incorporate Biblical principles into your financial life.

As I mentioned, early on in this pursuit I was not as familiar with God's Word as I thought I was. I was not well versed in Biblical truths. At this point you are probably far ahead of me, since you are likely reading this book because you want to integrate your faith and your finances to make a significant impact with your money.

In our professional lives, people only see about ten percent of the work we do as financial advisors. Most of the work we do for clients is behind the scenes. There are similar tools, techniques, and strategies that are used by many professionals, and it may, therefore, seem like all financial advisors are alike. But an advisor who employs a Biblical worldview can explore bigger and more important questions related to faith, stewardship, leaving a legacy, and bringing an eternal perspective.

Once I started understanding that life was about God and his purpose, not me and all I wanted to accomplish,

---

[6] Ron Blue, Kingdom Advisors Core Training Overview, session 2, page 1.

I knew I had an amazing opportunity to not only incorporate this wisdom into my own life, but also to share it with others. I realized that discipleship begins with me, and that by helping others through my work, I could continue to learn and grow in my own faith journey.

Keep putting into practice all you learned and received from me—everything you heard from me and saw me doing. Then the God of peace will be with you.
Philippians 4:9 (NLT)

You may be wondering how advice you receive from a Kingdom Advisor differs from the advice you might receive from any other financial advisor. As I mentioned, on the surface there are a lot of similarities. All advisors should be talking with you about your spending, debt, and taxes. Of course, they will talk to you about your margin—often urging you to invest all that is left.

Shortly we'll talk more about how Biblical investing differs from mainstream investing. But a very big difference for me was learning about the real meaning of stewardship, and incorporating that discussion into my client meetings. Before this journey, I never talked with clients about their giving, or the importance of tithing. Not as an act of judgment or guilt, but as a blessing. Not just a blessing to those we give to, but a blessing to us!

Clients often ask, "How do I tithe ten percent of my income, when I don't have anything left at the end of the month?" We're told to trust God, give him the first ten percent, and it will all work out. I can't explain exactly how it works, but for me, that's exactly what happened. Once we started tithing, we still always had enough to pay the bills and do what we needed to do. My colleagues and I have come to call this "the math problem" because we can't see how mathematically and logically this can possibly work! My life changed dramatically when I started tithing, and I love sharing that with clients.

For a specific example of Biblical wisdom in practice:

A secular advisor would likely set up an estate plan for you that makes sure your kids get the maximum amount of money and assets when you die.

Incorporating Biblical wisdom requires more in-depth and hard-hitting questions: Are your kids prepared to handle that kind of inheritance? Is it the wisest course of action? Are there other ministries you could support that would be more impactful and meaningful? These are tough questions to answer, but important when you are considering the best outcome for your family, and God's Kingdom.

Once I put in the work to learn Biblical principles, it was easier for me to move to believing that those principles were true, and that I could integrate them into my life. The struggle I had, and maybe you do, too, is the DOING. Incorporating these principles into my work and life meant significantly changing how I do business. I often refer to these verses from James:

But don't just listen to God's word. You must do what it says. Otherwise, you are only fooling yourselves. For if you listen to the word and don't obey, it is like glancing at your face in a mirror. You see yourself, walk away, and forget what you look like. But if you look carefully into the perfect law that sets you free, and if you do what it says and don't forget what you heard, then God will bless you for doing it.

James 1:22-25 (NLT)

After I completed the Core Curriculum, I went on to study a special Kingdom Advisors training program developed by Dan Hardt called *Biblically Responsible Investing: Understanding the Heart of God.*

It was in this program that I learned specifically about BRI, and that this type of investing is one more way I can show my love for the Lord. I had to consider that if I was investing in companies and business practices that are offensive to God, then I probably wasn't being a good steward of His money.

In the 1990's the phrase "What Would Jesus Do?" became popular as a standard for Christians to check their words and behavior. I think it applies here. If Jesus were walking the Earth with us today and participating in the rigors of work and saving for the future like we do today, what kind of business practices do you think He would support? I don't think this is such a wild question. I feel confident that Jesus would want to avoid the business practices that go against God's Word.

Understanding the Heart of God also helped me grasp many of the practical issues of building a BRI portfolio, such as different kinds of screening and which money managers employ these principles. Most importantly, it introduced me to the concept of the disciple-making BRI Advisor. I started to consider the great opportunities that practicing BRI would afford me in sharing what I was learning in my faith with the clients I served.

Chapter 4
Learning The Stock Market Game™

Investing is sometimes seen as a passive activity, but as a stockholder you are promoting and profiting from whatever a company does. If a company sells porn, you are encouraging and profiting from human weakness.
Tom Strobhar, Investment Advisor

At the same time that I was starting my "quest" and learning as much as I could about Biblically Responsible Investing, I also was teaching The Stock Market Game™ at my son's middle school. This is an educational curriculum for kids in elementary school through high school that teaches the basics of investing. Besides the classroom teaching, there is also a virtual investing activity. The kids are broken up into small groups and given a virtual portfolio of $100,000 to invest in stocks, bonds, and mutual funds. They compete against other schools in their region for significant prizes. Of course, the prizes go to those who make the most money over the course of the semester.

This was the second time I had taught The Stock Market Game™. I love to teach and make investing concepts easy for others. I believe if very young kids can learn and understand the basics of investing, anyone can!

When I went to teach the curriculum this particular time, the concepts hit me in a new way. I think the first time I glossed over many of the ideas because they seemed so basic to me.

I want to go over a very short version of those concepts for you here, because this experience really helped me to understand the concept of ownership in investing, as well as my responsibility in knowing what companies I own. I think this will help build a logical case about the significance of your investments.

What is a company?

A company is a business or association usually formed to manufacture or supply products or services for a profit. A company can be a sole proprietorship, partnership, or a corporation.[7]

So, why do companies exist in the first place? At a basic level, an entrepreneur has found a need that he or she can meet, and has come up with a solution that will

---

[7] What is a company?, The Stock Market Game, page 1

satisfy the needs of a customer group, with the hopes of bringing value to that group and solving a problem.

And, of course, there's the matter of making money. No one goes into business to lose money, or to break even. The owners of the company want to generate a profit.

You might be thinking, "What about nonprofit companies?" A nonprofit company functions just like any other company, with the exception of what it does with the profits. Many companies will take the profit and pay it out to the shareholders (owners). Nonprofit companies use the profits to further the mission or purpose of the company. The organization must provide some public benefit, as in the case of churches, hospitals, or schools.

Contrary to what many people believe, nonprofit organizations still want to, and in fact *need* to, make a profit to survive. They need to pay all of their bills, including employee salaries. The only difference is that instead of paying the profits to the shareholders, they keep the money to continue to grow the business.

Today, many companies have a goal of accomplishing some social good, and that's very admirable. But that is not a requirement of a company, and in fact, many companies do not have social goals in mind when they are formed.

Concept One: *The primary reason companies exist is to make a profit.*

What is a stock?

A stock is a share in the ownership of a publicly held company. In exchange for the money paid to purchase the stock, the stockholder can vote for the company's board of directors and benefit from its financial success.[8]

Once a company has become successful, the owners may decide to move from private ownership to public ownership. For example, if you own a family business, this means you would look for others to invest in your company and you would no longer be the sole owner. The first public sale of stock by a company is called an IPO, or initial public offering.

The reason a company issues stock is to raise money that it can use to expand or grow its business. The goal is for the business to become even more profitable.

There are a number of reasons a company might want to raise money by issuing stock:

- To develop new products
- To buy more advanced equipment
- To pay for new buildings and inventories
- To hire more employees
- To provide for a merger or acquisition

---

[8] ibid.

- To decrease debt
- To give company owners greater flexibility
- To place a market value on the company

Concept 2: *The only reason that companies issue stock is to raise money to grow their business.*

Quite literally, a stockholder is a part owner of the company. As an owner, you are entitled to your share of the company's earnings as well as any voting rights attached to the stock. The extent of the voting rights you have depends on what proportion of the stock you own.

Concept 3: *When you invest in the company, you become part owner. You get to vote on the officers and, in that sense, have a say in the company. How much say you have depends on how much you own.*

What is a mutual fund?

You might be thinking, "That sounds confusing. It's a good thing I don't own stocks—I only own mutual funds!" I hate to be the bearer of bad news, but you probably do own stocks, just in another way.

A mutual fund is a collection of stocks, bonds, and other securities owned by a group of investors and managed by a professional investment advisory firm. The investment advisor collects the money from the investors (that's you) and pools the money together to buy various stocks and bonds.[9]

Investing in mutual funds is a good way for you to diversify your portfolio so you are not exposed to the risks of owning just one or a few companies. Diversifying the risk over multiple investments means that if a company has a bad year, or goes out of business, it will not have as much of an impact on you.

Different funds have different objectives, ranging from conservative to very aggressive. There also may be special objectives, such as funds that are socially responsible or Biblically responsible.

The important thing to remember is that mutual funds are typically a big basket of stocks or bonds, and you own a little bit of all of them.

How does money grow over time?

Your investment portfolio really grows in two ways:

Appreciation: The value of the shares increases over time. If you bought one share of the XYZ Company for $10 (this is referred to as your **principal)** and later sold it for $20, you would have earned $10 in capital appreciation.

Dividends: If the company has had a good year, the

---

[9] ibid.

Board of Directors may decide to pay or increase a portion of the company's earnings to the stockholders. They can pay this dividend in cash or in shares of stock.

Concept 4: *The reason that people invest in the stock market is to make more money—to increase their wealth as the company grows and succeeds.*

If, as an investor, you are the owner of a company, it only makes sense you would own companies you love, or at the very least, agree with their business practices. Which brings us to a big problem: Very few investors actually understand what they own in their portfolios.

Why don't we know what we own?

If you are ever curious to learn about the history of stock trading, it's a pretty fascinating story which can be traced back at least as far as the 1300's in Venice. Even up to a few decades ago, you knew exactly what you were investing in when you purchased stock in a company. You very likely knew what business practices the company was involved in, and, if you thought it was a good business venture, you invested your hard-earned money in it.

There are many reasons the world of investing has become more complicated and murky in recent years. Here are just a few:

1. Companies today are involved in multiples lines of business. Companies such as General Electric (GE) have dozens of lines of business. It's hard to determine if you agree with their business practices. You may agree with some, and disagree with others.
2. Investment vehicles such as mutual funds and Exchange Traded Funds (ETFs) make it more difficult to know in which companies you are invested. If you own ten mutual funds, and each fund owns thirty to fifty company stocks, how could you possibly be expected to know and understand what you are invested in? The increasing number of layers and levels of complexity in these investments allows most investors and many financial advisors to ignore or distance themselves from the practices of a business, and focus solely on performance.
3. Many people employ a financial advisor to handle their investing. They ask very few questions, and leave it up to the advisor to make the decisions. You may have a conversation with your advisor about your values and what you do and do not want to invest in. The truth is, unless your advisor has special screening software, he probably is also unclear about the business practices in which you are investing. He may or may not admit that to you!

Many investors today have a singular focus—making money—with no consideration of HOW that money is being made.[10]

I no longer wanted to separate my faith and my business. I wanted to try to please God with my choice of investments, although at the time I really was not sure what that meant. To understand how this would all work, I had to break it down into small easy pieces, as I laid it out for you in the previous four concepts. Remember finance was not my first language, healthcare was. I think the language of finance is what makes it seem so confusing sometimes. Let's review the basics in four easy points:

1. The main reason companies exist is to make a profit. Even if they are "nonprofit" they cannot continue to operate unless they're making enough money to cover their expenses.
2. The reason companies issue stock is to raise money to grow their business—to do more of what they are already doing.
3. When you invest in the company, you become part owner. You get to vote on the officers and have a say in the company. How much say you have depends on how much you own.
4. This brings me back to point number one: The reason we invest (and own companies) is to make

---

[10] Finny Kuruvilla, PhD, Live presentation, "The Myths of Biblically Responsible Investing."

money.

This is where we need to bring it all together: When you invest in the company, whether it's a stock or mutual fund, you are quite literally saying, "Take my money and do more of what you're doing, and let's make a boat load of money together." You are hoping and praying that this company is successful so that you can benefit from it.

For example, if you are unknowingly invested in companies involved in the abortion industry, or abortion philanthropy, e.g., donors to Planned Parenthood, you are praying with your dollars these companies will prosper and perform more and more abortions so that your money grows.

Your reaction at this point might be, "I would never invest in those companies, and my nice Christian financial advisor would never invest in those companies, either." I am here to tell you unless your advisor specifically uses screening tools to choose investments or specifically hires money managers who implement BRI as part of their mandate, he or she does not have a clear understanding of all the business practices you are invested in.

Taking the time to understand how investing works at its most basic level started to give me clarity about the real meaning of stock ownership, and I wanted to learn more about what business practices I was invested in and profiting from.

Chapter 5
Aligning Your Values and Your Investments

A Christian should avoid investing in any enterprise that makes its profit from people doing what they shouldn't.

- Randy Alcorn,
Pastor and Author of *The Treasure Principle*

Every financial decision is a spiritual decision.
– Ron Blue, Founder of Kingdom Advisors

The Parable of the Talents
While many Christians are very familiar with Biblical teaching related to staying out of debt and being a cheerful giver, we do not necessarily think of Biblical wisdom regarding investing. You are probably familiar with the Parable of the Talents in Matthew 25: 14-30, but for our purposes I will summarize it here, in my own words:

A respected master decided to go on a journey so he

called three of his servants together to give them instructions on caring for his property while he was away. Based on their ability and experience, to the first servant he gave five talents, to the second servant he gave two talents, and to the third servant he gave one talent.

We don't know how long the master was away, but when he returned, he called the servants back together to see what they had accomplished in his absence and to settle accounts. The first servant used the money he had been given to grow the business and doubled his money, returning ten talents to the master. The second servant also doubled his money and returned four talents to the master. Of course, the master was pleased with his hundred percent return on investment and promised to increase the responsibilities of these two servants, because they had passed his test and proven themselves worthy of handling more.

The third servant, however, was fearful of losing the master's money so he had buried it in the ground. He figured he wouldn't gain anything, but as least he wouldn't lose anything, either. The master was furious! He called the third servant wicked and lazy, fired him on the spot, and told him to hit the road.

Take note of verse 27: *Why didn't you deposit my money in the bank? At least I would have gotten some interest on it.* (NLT)

"According to *New Nave's Topical Bible*, one who

possessed five talents of gold or silver was a multimillionaire by today's standards. Some calculate the talent in the parables to be equivalent to twenty years of wages for the common worker. Other scholars estimate more conservatively, valuing the New Testament talent somewhere between $1,000 to $30,000 dollars today."[11]

Here we are in the New Testament, and Jesus is talking about the benefits of investing and gaining interest! My takeaway from this passage is whether we are given a little or a lot, God expects us to make the most of what we have been given.

Why is the master so angry with the third servant? Plainly, the servant was not being a good steward of the master's money. In fact, he was being selfish, because all he really cared about was saving his own skin. He did not want to take the risk of losing the money, and therefore missed an opportunity to increase what he had been given.

As Christians I think we are sometimes convinced we should not want more. We are taught to be content with what we have, but there is a fine balance between contentment and making excuses so we can avoid what God has called us to do. Our time, talents, and treasures are not ours; they are God's, and we are just the

---

[11] Mary Fairchild, "What is a Talent?" About Religion, http://christianity.about.com/od/glossary/a/Talent.htm

caretakers. There is a price to be paid when we squander what we have been given.

The story makes me believe that Jesus would have us be investors. No matter what we are given—one talent or five—we should take whatever we have and multiply it, hopefully in ways that can be a blessing.

If we take this one Scripture and isolate it, you could come away thinking that God is saying, "Whoever makes the most money wins." After all, the first servant was not only rewarded with praise and more responsibility; he was also given the talent of the third servant. Of course, looking at one single passage of Scripture without looking at the greater context is never wise. So I pressed on.

The logical next question is, "Does God really care what companies I am invested in?" What I was really looking for was a Scripture passage that clearly said, "It's okay for you to invest in any company—I won't hold you responsible" or "And the Lord said not to invest in any company that profits from immoral activities." You know, black and white. A clear answer. To find an answer to this question, I had to integrate what I was learning about God's Word with the practicalities of investing in the secular world.

The truth is, while the Bible has a lot to say about this topic, it's not spelled out quite so literally. I had to go to several pieces of Scripture to cover all of my questions. I think for most immoral activities you could easily understand the Biblical basis for why we don't want to fund and profit from them.

I'm grateful to Dr. Finny Kuruvilla from Eventide Funds for laying out the logical order of these Scriptures for me. It helped me see Scripture itself builds a compelling argument for BRI. Let's look at what God says regarding investing in questionable business practices.[12]

Whether you eat or drink or whatever you do, do it all for the glory of God.

1 Corinthians 10:31 (NLT)

We should keep God first and foremost in every part of our lives, not just where it's convenient for us. I had to take a serious look at how I sometimes try to pick and choose what parts of my life are devoted to God, and what parts I will leave to the secular world, you know—hold onto for myself. The truth is, money did not fit into my idea of ways of glorifying God. In this verse, when you take it to heart and don't just gloss over it, you would say, "Yes of course, that's true. I want to do everything for the glory of God."

Now if I'm trying to glorify God with my money, and at the same time I'm invested in big companies and

---

[12] Finny Kuruvilla, PhD, Live presentation, "The Myths of Biblically Responsible Investing."

quite frankly at this point I don't even know what they are involved in, can God really hold me responsible? I think the following passage addresses this:

> *My child, if sinners entice you,*
> *turn your back on them!*
> *They may say, "Come and join us.*
> *Let's hide and kill someone!*
> *Just for fun, let's ambush the innocent!*
> *Let's swallow them alive, like the grave;*
> *let's swallow them whole, like those who go down to*
> *the pit of death.*
> *Think of the great things we'll get!*
> *We'll fill our houses with all the stuff we take.*
> *Come, throw in your lot with us;*
> *we'll all share the loot."*
> *My child, don't go along with them!*
> *Stay far away from their paths.*
> *They rush to commit evil deeds.*
> *They hurry to commit murder.*
> *If a bird sees a trap being set,*
> *it knows to stay away.*
> *But these people set an ambush for themselves;*
> *they are trying to get themselves killed.*
> *Such is the fate of all who are greedy for money;*
> *it robs them of life.*
>
> Proverbs 1:10-19 (NLT)

Let me give you an interpretation of this passage. This passage relates a father telling his son to use common sense: Don't get caught up in schemes with sinners. They will entice you with what appears to be fun, and get-rich-quick schemes. They will tell you how we will share in the profits together—come along with us and we will all get rich together. Don't get caught up with these bad characters. They are their own worst enemies. *If you associate with these bad fellows, you are just as bad as they are because you went along with it.* (This is where my mom would say, "If all your friends jumped off a bridge, would you do it, too?") It also says that if you try to acquire money dishonestly or illegally, you will suffer the consequences.

The New International Version of the Bible refers to this money as "ill-gotten gain," money or other possessions acquired in a dishonest or illegal fashion. In this passage the father is saying, "It doesn't matter if you started it or not, you'll be in just as much trouble for going along with it."

The thought of making big bucks in the market is pretty enticing. Anytime we can take a short-cut to success, we can be tempted. It is fun and makes us feel like part of the crowd. It is important not to make decisions on short-range promises, but in terms of the long-range effects. Sometimes we have to avoid being unequally yoked in our lives, in our business, and with our money. I think it is very important to be equally yoked with your financial advisor, so you can make good decisions together.

This passage also made me realize sometimes we try to push responsibility for decisions onto others: "I don't know what I'm investing in—it's whatever my advisor recommended to me." That might mean you just go along with whatever investments are recommended, and you might not really know what the companies are involved in. You also don't want to ask a lot of questions and be a pain about it, so you just go along with the plan, even though you do not understand it.

You should know there are relatively few financial advisors who know the specific activities of the companies that they invest in. I would guess there are very few advisors who can name the top three companies in which their clients are invested. As I mentioned before, investing has become an abstract concept and we have removed ourselves from the decision-making process.

Now what if you are making profits (and at this point you still do not know what activities they are coming from) but you decide just to be safe you will tithe the profits at church to offset any potential harm you may be doing? The Bible has something to say about that, too.

When you are bringing an offering to fulfill a vow, you must not bring to the house of the Lord your God any offering from the earnings of a prostitute, whether a man or a woman, for both are detestable to the Lord your God.

Deuteronomy 23:18 (NLT)

You cannot honor God with the profits you made from illegal or immoral activities. Since God hates those illegal activities, he hates those profits and anything associated with those activities. We have to ask ourselves, "Do I ever make the excuse that the end justifies the means?" God is telling us this is not true— he cares how we acquire our money even if we end up donating it all to charity.

This is a prime example of how we can make a significant impact with our money by really examining the activities of the companies that we invest in, and making a choice not to be unequally yoked. In a business sense that means you do not want to be in partnership with someone who has opposite worldviews and morals, because someone—often the Believer— gets pressured to abandon or compromise his principles for the sake of profit and business growth.

Don't be fooled by those who say such things, for "bad company corrupts good character."

1 Corinthians 15:33 (NLT)

That is a lesson I wish I had learned early on in my

life! It would have saved me a tremendous amount of heartbreak over the years.

If God doesn't want anything to do with the money we made from immoral activities—and I think He states it clearly in the Deuteronomy passage—I think the answer to the question, "Does God care what companies I invest in?" is a definite YES.

This is the point at which I found myself needing to make some decisions. When I worked in Organizational Development, I spent a number of years focused on developing and teaching the mission, vision, and values of the organization. I worked on a multitude of programs to evaluate employees on how they were embracing and living out our corporate values. I believe one of the most stressful things a person can experience is being forced to make a choice that goes against their beliefs.

The easiest example of this, which you may have experienced, is in the workplace. You or someone you know may have had the experience of working for a company or for a boss who has asked you to do something you are not comfortable with, because you know it's not right. This could involve how customers are treated, how the books are balanced, or perhaps the wrongful dismissal of an employee. The choice to stand up and do the right thing might lead to getting in trouble or even fired. If you have the courage to stand up and do the right thing, then bravo! However, I think many people, when faced with the dilemma of losing their job, would do whatever it takes to keep it.

Think about how you would feel afterwards as a result of consciously doing something that goes against your belief system. You would probably experience a gnawing at your gut, replaying the incident over and over, a constant unease that never quite seems to disappear. If you have personally had this experience, you know exactly what I am talking about.

Biblically Responsible Investing automatically aligns the way you invest God's money with Biblical principles. If I believe God is pro-life and I profess to be pro-life, yet I own and profit from companies that perform or support abortion, then I am not living in alignment with my values. If you don't *know* that you are profiting from companies that go against Biblical values and likely your own values– then that's one thing. But if armed with the knowledge you have today, you continue to invest that way, then you are making a conscious choice to live in conflict with your values.

While there were still many questions left to be answered, I knew that if I was going to recommit my life to Christ, I would have to implement some big changes in the way I did business. I could no longer invest in and profit from companies opposing Biblical principles. I also knew if I really believed what I had been learning, then I could not help my clients invest in these companies, either.

Learning What I Owned

Of course, the next step was to discover exactly what companies I was investing in and what those companies were doing. Some business practices are obvious, and some are not. I was shocked to discover I was unknowingly profiting from businesses engaged in or promoting abortion, pornography, anti-family causes, and many other practices I was against. My research revealed $.38 of every dollar in mutual funds and managed money is invested in these practices I oppose.[13] I became convinced I had to not only change the way I was personally investing, but had to help others understand the impact of their investing choices.

At this point you might be thinking, "I don't even *want* to know what I'm investing in!" The truth, though, is you probably really do care. Just as people who are passionate about the environment often invest in Socially Responsible funds, you should know what you are investing in and how that aligns with your faith values.

Since you are still with me, we can assume you feel passionate about certain conservative issues including abortion and pornography. How would it impact you to know approximately forty percent of the companies in

---

[13]BRI Institute.

the S&P 500 are, in fact, funding business practices like these that you oppose? You may be supporting charitable causes that align with your faith values, and at the same time your investment dollars are undermining your good intentions. For example, Planned Parenthood receives a significant portion of its funding from corporate America.[14]

By now you are probably curious to know exactly what the businesses in your portfolio support. In Chapter 10 I will share some practical steps so you can find out exactly what your investment dollars are funding in your personal portfolio.

To do this properly you must have your portfolio screened. Financial advisors who offer special types of investing including Socially Responsible Investing or Biblically Responsible Investing have software programs in which they can input the specific stocks and mutual funds in your portfolio, and produce an individualized report so you can see exactly where your investment dollars are going.

You might be saying, "I don't want to screen my portfolio because I'm afraid of what I'll find and then I will actually have to do something about it." If this is you, then keep on reading because in the next chapter I will address frequently asked questions—and yes, even objections—to investing in a Biblically responsible way!

---

[14] Planned Parenthood Annual Report 2013-2014

Chapter 6
Why you THINK You Can't Implement BRI

Stay away from every kind of evil.
1 Thessalonians 5:22 (NLT)

By now you may be thinking, "investing in this way just makes sense." The big question is: If BRI is such a great idea, why have you not heard of it, and the bigger question—why aren't all Christians doing this already?

I think many of us, when something comes into our life we do not really understand, we put on our blinders, and maybe even hope it goes away. Then we won't have to deal with it. Often I find I cannot completely ignore issues or facts once I have learned them. They burrow deep into my mind until I pay attention to them. That's why I had to go on this journey—I couldn't be at peace until I had some answers!

One reason Christians may not be investing in this way is because they do not know about it. That is a pretty valid reason. After reading this book, though, you will no longer have that excuse!

I found most people assume if their financial advisor is Christian, they already invest in this way. In many cases, this is simply not true. There are extra steps advisors must take to implement a screening process so they know which companies not to invest in, and many advisors do not feel compelled to take those extra steps.

Now you know about Biblically Responsible Investing. What other roadblocks do you have about investing in this way? I will share some very good questions that I have heard from clients, and my answers. I hope you will pray about it.

I am not a financial advisor. In fact, I do not really understand investing at all. I cannot be held responsible for where my money is invested.

At the heart of this argument is the issue of responsibility. You may think, "Seriously now, I cannot control or be responsible for what big companies do. They are going to have to answer to God for that—not me." Can we really be held responsible for the actions of companies?

Take no part in the worthless deeds of evil and darkness, instead expose them.

Ephesians 5:11 (NLT)

As part owners I do think we have a responsibility to

know what our companies are doing so we can make informed choices. Previously we talked about not becoming caught in schemes and just going along with them. Now that you know there is another way to invest, what would your answer be on Judgment Day? "I knew I was probably profiting from businesses You oppose, but You can't hold me responsible for that." It sounds like a weak argument to me.

I am not one to challenge and debate others, but I am convicted on this point: You have the responsibility to make good choices for you, your family, and the Kingdom. It may seem overwhelming, but in Chapter 10 I will lay out an easy action plan for you to follow.

Isn't this all a little "over the top?" No company is perfect. Every company has some sin in it.

The investment world in which we willingly participate supports both good and bad activities, and we need to be responsible for our investments.

Just because we cannot remove all sin from a portfolio does not mean we should not try. That standard of perfection does not apply in any other area of life. For instance, when your kids learn a new skill, do you say, "You can't do it perfectly, so you should quit?" Perfection is not the only sign of progress. We can move in a very positive direction even though perfection probably is not going to be the outcome. Obviously, there is subjectivity in the process. At this point there is no clear consensus on a standard of BRI, and I think that's fine. The same holds true for the Socially Responsible Investing movement, but those investors have jumped in and supported the movement, helping it to grow exponentially.

Just because there is subjective judgment, it doesn't invalidate the process. All advisors use subjective judgment in what we select in our portfolios, and I know we have all kinds of objectives standards, criteria, and rules we try to follow. Oftentimes, when it comes down to options A and B, it becomes a judgment call. It is best to look to Scripture, pray, seek guidance from godly advisors who have already been doing it, establish a standard, and do your best to adhere to it. Some people only have a negative standard, in which they screen out things such as abortion and pornography, alcohol, tobacco, gambling, etc. Others do both a negative and a positive screening in which they proactively search for companies fitting certain positive criteria.

Some people only care about the products and services companies provide but others want to do that *plus* they look at corporate activism, meaning they look at what are they are doing with their profits and what causes they promote. Having subjectivity means becoming involved and starting to understand the issues and applying your own spirit-led judgment. That does not invalidate BRI.

When evaluating any given company, if you

interviewed twenty BRI advisors, you would find *something* negative. It will never be perfect. If we excluded every bit of imperfection, we would have to exclude ourselves, and we would not have anything left to invest in. There are no perfect people, therefore, there are no perfect companies. What we are looking for are companies that try to add value to society, without extracting from it.

In other words, start somewhere. It does not have to be perfect. You do not have to know all the rules and all the definitions. You can just pick something that is very compelling to you. Perhaps it is screening out abortion. Start someplace and allow it to grow from there.

What is the difference between boycotting a company and not investing in it?

You are asking about the difference in being a consumer of a company's products and being an owner of the company. A consumer is a person who purchases goods and services for personal use. In Chapter 4 I covered what it means to be an owner. Either one, or both, of these strategies can be used to impact the business.

Here is the difference for me: As a consumer, you are enjoying the products of the company for your personal use. When you are an owner of the company, you participate in the company's profits.

If a tobacco company is making profits by

encouraging young children in Third World countries to become addicted to cigarettes, I do not want to profit from that. I do not want to receive a big dividend knowing where that money came from.

A very important point on both of these boycotting strategies is you need large numbers of people acting together in order to make a difference. If you stage your own personal boycott, you will not have much of an impact. However, if you can get everyone who feels the same way you do to act en masse, then you have yourself a movement.

Think back to August 1, 2012. Proponents of same-sex marriage called for a boycott of Chik-fil-A after Dan Cathy, the company CEO, caused an uproar when he said his company endorsed the "Biblical definition of the family unit."

Mike Huckabee encouraged a *counter*-boycott in order to support a business that operates on Christian principles. On August 1, thousands of people flocked to the restaurants to show their support. As a result, Chik-fil-A had a record- setting day in sales. This is the kind of support we need to cultivate in the Christian community to rally for the values we hold dear.

I think this is a great idea, but really, it is just one more thing on my to-do list. Aren't I already doing enough?

You say, "I am allowed to do anything"—but not everything is good for you. You say, "I am allowed to do anything"—but not everything is beneficial.

1 Corinthians 10:23 (NLT)

You may be thinking, "Aren't I doing enough already? I go to church, I read my Bible, I teach Sunday School, and I volunteer. Where do I draw the line?" All of those things are great, and I do not want to take away from any of them. This is where I had to go back to that concept of making all the parts of my life integrated.

I wanted to make my money matter, and to do that I had to include my finances—not pick and choose the parts of my life I wanted to exclude.

Try not to view BRI as "one more thing" on your checklist. I encourage you to learn as much as you can in an attempt to align your money with your values. You might be surprised! What started as an overwhelming journey of discovery for me blessed me in unexpected ways I could never have imagined.

My financial advisor is a Christian, a very nice fellow, and he would *never* invest in those kinds of companies. I am sure he is already investing this way.

If your financial advisor is already investing for you in Biblically responsible funds and companies, that is terrific news! Can you truly answer the following questions?

- How do you know?
- How did your advisor talk about it with you?
- How did they explain it to you?
- What exactly is their screening process?

The truth is most advisors, including Christian advisors, have not thought about it. If you are making an assumption your advisor is doing this, I have some bad news and some good news for you.

The bad news is if your advisor has not talked to you about this, or if he can't articulate his position and screening process clearly, he is not doing it. You may think, "I don't want to ask, because I don't want to know." We are too far along in this discussion for excuses!

Here is the really good news: Many Christian financial advisors say they have not implemented BRI because their clients haven't asked for it. Now, we both know most investors do not even know to ask these questions, but let's cut your financial advisor some slack. This is your big opportunity to talk to your financial advisor about BRI, what you have learned, and its importance. You can be the catalyst that motivates your financial advisor to start investing in this way, not only for you, but also for his other clients.

Many people wrongly assume you have to change financial advisors to implement BRI.

I think this is a great idea, but my financial advisor is my (uncle, cousin, brother-in-law, best friend from high school, etc.), and I can't change financial advisors and also preserve that relationship.

Don't team up with those who are unbelievers. How can righteousness be a partner with wickedness? How can light live with darkness?
                                        2 Corinthians 6:14 (NLT)

Think about your motive in implementing BRI. In Scripture we see over and over where God introduces circumstances, not because he needs to know what is in our heart, but so our heart can come out. This is an opportunity for you to have a conversation with your financial advisor about BRI. How open do you think your advisor would be to learning about BRI and implementing this in your portfolio? I have heard many stories of advisors learning about—and then becoming convicted about—BRI, because they had a client who demanded it. By nature, advisors want to make you happy.

BRI is not a market strategy for gaining assets. I will speak for the advisors who are investing according to BRI principles. We would LOVE to continually add new advisors to our ranks! We are about serving people and looking out for their best interests.

It carries so much more impact when you can help change an advisor's heart and perspective on this issue. The opportunities created by doing that, as opposed to just gathering more assets for our firm, are tremendous.

If, after your initial conversation, the family or friend or your best friend advisor is not interested in learning more, it comes down to a judgment call for you. What are you going to prioritize—living your faith values or avoiding a conflict with your advisor?

As Buck Jacobs, Founder of the C12 Group, would say, "What are you going to put first: your friend's feelings or Jesus?" I have never felt bold enough to say that until now.

I invest in my denomination's funds, so I am confident I am not investing in these kinds of negative business practices.

I will keep this short and sweet, but suffice it to say that just because you are invested in the funds of your denomination, it does not mean they would pass Biblically responsible screens. Why not? I am not sure. BRI is not something most financial managers have considered. Some denominations report a portion of their funds are screened, but they typically include many funds that would be excluded based on our discussion thus far.

I encourage you to find out more. The message here is do not make assumptions—ask good questions. The easiest thing to do is to get your portfolio screened, and then you will know in what business practices you are invested.

Questions for Financial Advisors:
Why you THINK you cannot implement BRI
The following questions are specifically for financial advisors.

How do I introduce the topic of BRI to my clients when I have never talked with them about their faith?
Many advisors are concerned if they bring up the topic of faith with their clients, it will be a turn-off or they will be offended. At our firm we only practice Biblically Responsible Investing and have made this part of our formal discovery process, which we call the Vision Clarifier™. We start out a values-based discussion with every perspective client, which includes the BRI subject. I believe we must ask this question because it is our responsibility as a fiduciary. The conversation begins as follows:

"Are there any specific companies or industries you would prefer not to own in your portfolio due to faith or other reasons?"

Depending on the response we lead the discussion in

one of two ways. Either we confirm their moral concerns in investing in certain companies and have a direct conversation about how we implement BRI at our firm, or, if they seem less responsive, we focus on the positives of BRI. We explain why we preferentially seek to own companies creating positive changes in the world by living out the Golden Rule. This approach and this type of messaging is much more compelling and winsome, and who can argue with that?

When a client buys into this, they are not just buying into an allocation; they are affirming the core values they already hold dear. If they do not like these values, they are not going to like BRI. If they are your client, at worst they are ambivalent towards your values, or at best they are with you because they love those shared values. That being the case, you are now able to provide a different level of relationship other than only offering investment advice.

Prospective clients have said to me, "I don't really care about that." I go on to explain that even though they don't feel strongly about these business practices, it is the only way we invest. I have many non-Christian and non-conservative clients stick with us because they respect our position and because we are very good at what we do. Our goal is not to be a good Christian financial advisors, but to display excellence in how we do our work. Having an excellent advisor is something everyone is looking for.

My clients have not requested BRI, so they must not be interested in it.

If you are positioning yourself as a Christian advisor, your clients already assume you are doing BRI. Every single person I have ever talked to about BRI who has a Christian advisor replied to me, "My financial advisor is a Christian, so they are already investing this way." Can you imagine how they would feel if they have their portfolio screened and see what they are actually invested in? How do you defend that and maintain your client's trust?

It is much wiser to tell your clients you are learning about BRI, and are starting to implement it and offer these services to your clients. They will respect you more than if they find out this information on their own.

There is no clear-cut definition of BRI. Fund companies screen out businesses using different criteria. It is too murky for me.

I find this to be an interesting argument, because the Socially Responsible Investing movement does not seem to be suffering from this problem. Money invested in SRI funds is in the TRILLIONS. Yet each company has different screens or focal point for their funds.

On the other end of the spectrum, some advisors would say BRI is too "legalistic."

According to Brady Boyd, Pastor of New Life

Church in Colorado Springs,

"Legalism is believing God is demanding something impossible of us, something we'll never in a million years achieve. It is the bar set too high, the speed set too fast, the expectations set too lofty, the boundaries set too tight. It is a spiritual suffocation. It is darkness when we're desperate for light."[15]

I believe BRI is a balance between these two opinions, a strong framework for decision making with some room to breathe. Start by picking a screen you are most passionate about. Many advisors assume this is a black and white issue and you have to be all-out or all-in to this investing style. *Start somewhere.* Any time I have wanted to move my client's funds to a new portfolio, I move my money there first. It is how I can see how the fund or portfolio will work before I put someone else's money at risk.

I hope that after reading about BRI you will invest your own funds in a BRI portfolio so you can start to learn more and gain some confidence in this style of investing.

What if you buy stock on the secondary market? You cannot really say you are profiting from a business unless you participate in the Initial Public

---

[15] Brady Boyd, *Addicted to Busy,* p.142

Offering of the stock.

While this may be true concerning your initial purchase, it does not address the fact you are still profiting from the business in the form of capital appreciation and dividends.

In Matthew 27, after Judas had betrayed Jesus and felt guilty, he went to the priests to return the money.

The leading priests picked up the coins. "It wouldn't be right to put this money in the Temple treasury," they said, "since it was payment for murder."

Matthew 27:6 (NLT)

While the priests felt no guilt in paying Judas to betray Jesus, they would not accept the money when he returned it, because they said it was "blood money."

I am not trying to say investing in an immoral company equates to the murder of Jesus. I am saying if a company makes money by performing abortions, or by making the equipment used to perform abortions, I choose not to profit from it any way.

If I start investing this way, I will lose every single client I have, and I will never gain another client in my career.

This question was a very real part of my journey. I was convinced all of my clients would leave if I started investing this way. When I made the change, I only knew two of my clients were Christians. That would leave me with a very small book of business!

I was very anxious and fearful about this transition. There were times I was in tears knowing this would be the end of my business. (Have I built up enough drama for you yet?) Well, it is true. I was panicked. However, at the same time, I heard God's small, still, reassuring whisper. I absolutely knew this was what he was asking me to do.

When I finally decided not only would I invest my money this way, but that this is the only way that I would invest money for my clients, I sat down and had the conversation with each and every client. I gave them a choice to decide if they would embark on this new journey of Biblically Responsible Investing with me or choose to find a new advisor. You know what? In the end, I only lost two clients who were not on board with this approach to investing. I kept my Jewish clients, and even my liberal ones. The worst thing that happened was when a very good attorney friend who had been referring business to me heard I was doing BRI, she told me how embarrassed she was. That ended our business relationship, and, honestly, our friendship. Interestingly, the clients she referred are still with me. God has provided and blessed us with many new clients, far outweighing what I would have received in referrals from her.

I have walked through this change with several

advisors, and truthfully, everyone has the same fears. If you were to commit your business to God, and honor Him by investing in companies He is proud of, why wouldn't He bless that? I can tell you story after story of advisors who pushed through their fears and started offering BRI, only to look back on it as the best decision they have ever made. On the contrary, I do not know one story in which an advisor made this change and regretted the decision. Sometimes it is hard to take that leap of faith, but it is the best thing I have ever done in my business life.

The key ingredient in making a successful transition to doing BRI is motivation. Are we doing and operating and communicating from a position of love? Is that why we are doing this? You are not going to guilt or shame people into doing BRI in the same way you are not going to get many people to have a genuine relationship with Christ in that manner. It is about love, and it is about relationships and building from that place of love.

The final point is, there are great things happening in this space. Talented money managers are emerging, there is lot of teaching and growing in Christ that I see, and I do not want you to miss out on it!

Doesn't it make more sense to own shares in the companies you oppose so, as an owner, you can be a force for change in that company?

It is true there are two ways that you can practice

BRI. The first way is to divest of all the companies that oppose your faith values. The second way is to own a few shares of those companies so you can *protest* their business practices at shareholder meetings. Tom Strobhar, Founder of www.CorporateMorality.org, is famous for doing just that: Fighting big corporations on their business practices.

I have the greatest admiration for this approach! I will admit that I do not personally feel prepared to debate high level corporate officers about their business practices. If you do, please go ahead and do that! However, you cannot say it makes more sense to hold the stock and fight the company, and then hold the stock and *not* fight the company. What have you achieved? You have made a good point, but you have done nothing personally to contribute to the change in business practices we so desperately need.

In the next chapter we'll address what is probably your biggest concern about implementing BRI in your financial practice: BRI stock and fund performance.

Chapter 7
Can I Really Make Money Investing This Way?

Better a little, with godliness, than to be rich and dishonest.

Proverbs 16:8 (NLT)

One topic we have not touched upon is the challenges that surround talking about money in the church. In recent years, the "prosperity gospel" has emerged (also called the "health and wealth" gospel, or "name it and claim it"), basically saying God wants you to be rich.

Here is a more extensive description from The Gospel Coalition:

"No matter what name is used, the essence of this message is the same. Simply put, this 'prosperity gospel' teaches that God wants believers to be physically healthy, materially wealthy, and personally happy. Listen to the words of Robert Tilton, one of its best-known spokesmen: "I believe that it is the will of God for all to prosper because I see it in the Word, not because it has worked mightily for someone else. I do not put my eyes on men, but on God who gives me the power to get wealth." Teachers of the prosperity gospel encourage their followers to pray for and even demand material flourishing from God."[16]

Biblically Responsible Investing is not the prosperity gospel. It does not guarantee if you invest in God-honoring companies you will become rich. I want to make that point clear.

More likely, though, you are worried you will not make *any* money. I wish I could say I did not care about this aspect of Biblically Responsible Investing. You would think I am so far along in this journey, and so convinced this is the way God would have us invest, that this issue would not matter to me. The truth is I feel a strong responsibility to my clients, and I could not in good conscience try and convince them about this new way of investing if I thought they would lose money.

I have a few resources I will share with you about this. Before I do, here is a hypothetical example. You have the choice of investing in two different companies: one provides adult escort services and the other is a utility company. The first company promises a ten

---

[16] David W. Jones., "5 Errors of the Prosperity Gospel," The Gospel Coalition, June 5, 2015, http://www.thegospelcoalition.org/article/5-errors-of-the-prosperity-gospel

percent return on your money. The second company promises a five percent return on your money. Based on the assumption you share my faith values, and that even if you could double your return, you would not want to invest in an escort company. You are probably already learning you do care about more than just returns—you care about *how* you are making money.

With that example, you might think I am setting you up for a big disappointment, but that is not the case. I have two separate resources to share on this topic.

The first source of data is the accompanying slide from the BRI Institute. In this example, each year Rusty Leonard of the BRI Institute does a "back test" on the S&P 500. He looks at all 500 companies in the S&P 500 and classifies them as "Saints" and "Sinners." (The labels make me chuckle every time I think about it, but they are accurate!) Companies who are "saints" would pass typical BRI screens, and sinners would not. The "sinners" may be in violation of only one screen or, more likely in these large companies, several different screens.

After separating these two groups of companies, he runs data on how, as a group, they would have performed over the last ten years.

BRI Screened Portfolio Beats the S&P 500
Cumulative Returns of BRI Screened Portfolio vs. S&P 500
1/1/2000 – 9/30/2015

BRI Screened Portfolio
83.14%

S&P 500
76.62%

120%
100%
80%
60%
40%
20%
0%
-20%
-40%
-60%

2000
2003
2006
2009
2012
2015

Source: Stewardship Partners, Bloomberg

83

The graph on the previous page is:

BRI Back Test Source: Bloomberg, Stewardship Partners

The screened results presented in this chart are simulated and do not correspond to any real investment product. Simulated performance data are hypothetical and provided for informational purposes only. It does not reflect actual performance and is gross of any fees. This document is not an offer to buy or sell securities. Past performance is not indicative of future results. The number of companies screened out of the S&P 500 during the test period ranged from a low of 72 to a more recent high of 210 (out of 500). [17] Performance figures do not reflect the deduction of Investment Advisory Fees.

The takeaway from looking at this data is sometimes the "saints" were a little ahead, and sometimes the "sinners" were a little bit ahead. For the most part, though, they were always in the same ballpark.

While no one can predict future returns, this gave me some level of confidence we would not be sacrificing performance with our BRI screening approach. And, from the earlier hypothetical example, you probably decided you do not want to own those "sinners" anyway. Hopefully by now you are becoming comfortable with the idea you *can* invest in God-honoring companies without sacrificing returns.

I have a second resource. The Christian Investment Forum released a study in May of 2015 entitled "A Research Study on CIF Funds Composite Performance Relative to Industry Averages."

Here is an abstract of that study that briefly

---

[17] Stewardship Partners, "When Screening for Investments for Christian Values, Does Sin Win?" http://briinstitute.com/backtest.pdf

summarizes the findings:

"The **Christian Investment Forum** recently analyzed the performance of Biblically Responsible Investing funds from CIF Members and compared composites of those funds to the mutual fund industry averages across categories.

"The purpose of the study was not to identify or rate any single fund or portfolio manager as superior, but rather to test the concept that Biblically Responsible Investing screening has a similar relationship to performance as other screened investment approaches. Other firms and researchers have done performance relationship research for Socially Responsible Investing, but it has not been done on the related but distinct sector of Faith based investing. It is the hope of the Christian Investment Forum that others may follow with additional academic research in this specific area of investing.

"The results showed that Composite averages of CIF funds performed very similarly to the broad equity and bond categories. In three specific categories where there were sufficient CIF funds for analysis, the composite of CIF funds outperformed the industry average in all three.

"The results of this analysis are not meant to suggest that BRI funds will result in out-performance. **The most important reason to incorporate BRI funds into an**

overall investment portfolio is to better align investments with an investor's values. For investors and their advisors, considering funds that can align with their Christian faith need not be a choice between their values and performance."[18]

To download the white paper and read more details of this study follow this link: http://christianinvestmentforum.org/about-us/cif_research_composite funds.

It is my belief that by having some hard data you will gain some peace about performance issues surrounding BRI. I always recommend discussing the specifics of your investments with your financial advisor.

If you share my conservative Christian values, and yet you are still not convinced in the power of Biblically Responsible Investing, I have one question for you:

Why are you fighting so hard to rationalize investing in a company that goes against your beliefs? What are you trying to hold on to?

I encourage you to pray on that topic, and see what God reveals to you in terms of next steps for your faith and your business.

In the next chapter I cover what I think is a very exciting idea: What if all Christians and Christian financial advisors invested this way?

---

[18] John Silverling, "A Research Study on CIF Funds Composite Performance Relative to Industry Averages," May 2015.

Chapter 8

How Your Investments Can Make a Difference

If you are faithful in little things, you will be faithful in large ones. But if you are dishonest in little things, you won't be honest with greater responsibilities. And if you are untrustworthy about worldly wealth, who will trust you with the true riches of heaven?

Luke 16:10-11 (NLT)

Now step back for a moment and look at the bigger picture. I shared with you my spiritual and financial revelations along this journey. This issue is so much bigger than only one person. I wonder, "How would businesses look different if Christian investors only invested in stocks of companies demonstrating the values and virtues laid out in the Bible?"

Often we don't take action or make changes because we think we cannot make a difference in the world. Think about the power of grassroots revolutions. We all know great changes in the world are often started by tiny groups of people who have had an outsized effect. Can you imagine how exciting it would be to start a movement of Christian and conservative investors who wanted to make a change in the way we do business?

In "The Disciple Making BRI-Advisor," a module of the Kingdom Advisors BRI training course, Dan Hardt shares it was Christian investors who played a role in ending apartheid through shareholder activism and negative screening.[19]

Through the teaching of Dr. Finny Kuruvilla and his presentation, *"The Myths of Biblically Responsible Investing,"* I realized there are many examples of individuals and small groups working together to make a change, often resulting in an outsized effect. Some clear examples he shared include:

- The end of slavery in America, started by the efforts of Charles Finney and William Lloyd Garrison
- The ACLU, a small group who has had an enormous impact on our laws
- Hollywood has a significant influence on our culture and politics
- World Vision started with one man trying to help one child in one country with just $5. Today it helps more than 4 million children in nearly 100

---

[19] Dan Hardt, "The Disciple Making BRI-Advisor," a module of the Kingdom Advisors BRI training course

countries.[20]

One of my favorite illustrations is Greenpeace. I am intrigued by this example because they spawned the social responsibility movement, which later inspired the Socially Responsible Investing movement, which is much farther along in growth and acceptance than the BRI movement.

In a paragraph from the Greenpeace website: "In 1971, motivated by their vision of a green and peaceful world, a small team of activists set sail from Vancouver, Canada in an old fishing boat. These activists, the founders of Greenpeace, believed a few individuals can make a difference."[21]

Today, all of the largest companies in America report on their "green" initiatives and their carbon footprint. Greenpeace was started by a few people on a boat trying to save sea life, and that was only forty years ago. This example tells me if I start to invest this way and share the story with other Christians, then we, too, can make a difference.

Do I really believe we can make this happen? Yes, I do! In March of 2013 the mini-series *The Bible* broke viewing records on the History Channel. The premier was seen by 13.1 million viewers and currently ranks as

---

[20] "Our History," World Vision, http://www.worldvision.org/about-us/our-history

[21] "The History of Greenpeace," Greenpeace, http://www.greenpeace.org/seasia/ph/About-us/History/

cable's most- watched entertainment telecast of the year. That tells me there is a faction of people who can make this happen— surely more than would fit in a fishing boat!

While Biblically Responsible Investing (BRI) has yet to reach critical mass, we believe when those who share our beliefs band together and invest in the same way, we are voting and praying with our money to bless and grow God-honoring companies, and we will have the same ability to change business. As an example, imagine the impact of all Christians banding together and moving their investments from companies that oppose their faith values (abortion, pornography, and addictions, to name a few) and instead funding companies generous to their employees and seeking to cure diseases and improve our future by creating blessings in the world?

How can we start a grassroots revolution?
1. It begins with thinking (head knowledge)—knowing there is a way you can invest that also glorifies God.
2. The second step is believing (heart knowledge)— developing a personal conviction this is the way God would have you invest his money.
3. Next is doing—taking action and actually investing in ways that will, in essence, cut off the economic oxygen to certain companies, while growing those in alignment with our values.

4. Finally, sharing the word and telling those in your circle of influence about BRI and helping them learn the truth about their investments.

I am very passionate about the BRI movement. While the pioneers of this crusade have been at it for two decades, I am excited to contribute to something I believe is a very important part of our faith.

Here is what I know for sure: The only way that we will make a difference in these business practices is to develop a coordinated and determined effort towards those means. Chapter 10 details an Action Plan for steps to take to be a part of this significant movement.

Part III
Where Do We Go From Here?

Chapter 9
The Rest of the Story

God has given each of you a gift from his great variety of spiritual gifts. Use them well to serve one another.

1 Peter 4:10 (NLT)

As you now know, based on the facts that I shared with you and what I learned from God's Word, I discovered that I really was profiting from activities upon which God would not look favorably. I did marry Rick, and we did end up merging our companies–we call it our "Marriage and Acquisition."

Much has changed for me in the last few years since completing my "quest."

I have become an enthusiastic Bible reader. This has given me clarity on the issues God cares about. I always thought I knew the Bible because I knew the stories I heard growing up in Sunday School. My journey forced me to dig into the Bible and start to really try to understand God's Word and life lessons for me. I no longer think of God as the judgmental and punishing Father. I now see Jesus as a role model I want to follow and imitate to the best of my ability. I learned the grace I have received by Jesus' death on the cross is available to everyone once you are ready to accept it.

Knowing so much more now, I am confident I *don't* know the Bible, but it is my goal to keep learning and trying to understand more. It is how I feel closest to God.

I also feel I now have something to stand for. Before I was a chameleon, able to fit into any situation with any group of people with any set of beliefs and blend in with the crowd. I have become confident in my convictions as a Christ follower, and I am willing to defend my beliefs when necessary.

I have also become more enthusiastic about my work! I love being able to live out my faith through my business. One of my favorite meetings each week is my Tuesday morning call with the entire company when we not only discuss our successes, but also share devotions and pray together for our clients.

I used to feel enveloped by the negativity that often comes with my profession. Now I feel I can really help people understand on a basic level how they, too, can use their money to make a significant difference by making informed choices about their investments so they can glorify God. I love sharing Scripture with our clients and giving them clarity about their financial plans and investments.

Finally, I have great peace of mind about my own investments. I became convicted I will not profit from companies that go against God's Word. Of all the very hard choices I have made trying to act more like Jesus, investing in this way was the easiest one I have made. Practicing BRI is not a chore or a legalistic duty for me, it is a delight!

It is a struggle to feel as if you are living a compartmentalized life. I feel confident about my own choices and can now focus on the (many!) other areas of my life that still need work.

That deep emptiness that had gnawed at me for most of my life has subsided. I still have challenging days, as we all do. Things I thought were so important—more money, a bigger house, and striving to meet an impossible standard of "perfect"—do not seem so significant anymore. I am secure in knowing God has a plan for my life and everything I need will be provided. Each time I find myself worrying, I meditate on one of my favorite Scripture passages:

So be strong and courageous! Do not be afraid and do not panic before them. For the Lord your God will personally go ahead of you. He will neither fail you nor abandon you.

Deuteronomy 31:6 (NLT)

Along my journey I have surrounded myself with great role models, who show me what it looks like to live into my purpose.

While I have only been implementing BRI for a couple of years, I now serve as the leader of the BRI Special Interest Group at Kingdom Advisors. I love having the opportunity to provide educational opportunities for my fellow advisors as we grow this movement together.

I smile when I look back on the beginning of this journey. I wanted to keep my faith private. I was too self-conscious to even bless a meal in public. I now lead a Christian Business Women's Connection group where we meet and pray in public and encourage other businesswomen in the marketplace to join us. At a recent C12 Group meeting, I was encouraged to share my testimony. I would never have imagined I would have the courage to publically share my faith story. And now you hold it in your hands.

Chapter 10
Investor Action Plan

All Scripture is inspired by God and is useful to teach us what is true and to make us realize what is wrong in our lives. It corrects us when we are wrong and teaches us to do what is right. God uses it to prepare and equip his people to do every good work.

2 Timothy 3:16-17 (NLT)

My goal in writing this book was to share my personal journey back to my Christian roots, and to help lift the fog surrounding faith and investing. It is something we rarely pay attention to, but I hope you will continue to learn more in order to align your investments with your faith.

At this point you may be grappling with a whole lot of information you never knew, or never gave much thought to before. You may be wondering, "What in the world am I supposed to do now? I do not know what I am investing in, and I really do not know how to find out. What is the logical, but easy and unintimidating, next step for me?"

The biggest challenge that you now face is you will have the best intentions on taking these actions, but your hectic lifestyle will be a distraction and it will fall to the bottom of your to-do pile.

But don't just listen to God's Word. You must do what it says. Otherwise, you are only fooling yourselves.
James 1:22 (NLT)

This passage says that it is not enough to know God's Word, or even to believe it to be true; you also have to take action and do what you know God would have you do. Nothing else counts. Or, as one of my favorite authors, Lysa Terkeurst says, "Whatever God says do, do it. That's it. That is the entire Bible, Old Testament and New, hundreds of pages, thousands of verses, all wrapped up in six words."[22]

In the beginning of this book, I shared the process of knowing and believing something before we can take action on it. Well, it is not enough to know about BRI, and it is not enough to believe it is the right thing to do. Until you take action, nothing will change. The fastest

---

[22] Lysa TerKeurst, *What Happens When Women Say Yes to God: Experiencing Life in Extraordinary Ways,* page 20.

growing assets are the left-leaning Socially Responsible funds and Muslim-based funds. It is time for us to band together to support God-honoring companies and defund the business practices we oppose.

Step One: Pray

If you need wisdom, ask our generous God, and he will give it to you. He will not rebuke you for asking.

James 1:5 (NLT)

The first thing you can do is to pray for clarity on how God would have you invest His money. You might pray like this:

God, you have blessed me generously with far more than I deserve. I know that what I own doesn't really belong to me, it all belongs to you. Lord, what would you have me do with all you've entrusted to me? I long to do your will. As I am learning about Biblically Responsible Investing, please open my heart and my mind to hear your clear message. Amen.

Step Two: Continue to learn

So be careful how you live. Don't live like fools, but like those who are wise. Make the most of every opportunity in these evil days. Don't act thoughtlessly, but understand what the Lord wants you to do.

Ephesians 5:15-17 (NLT)

I shared many resources with you and have included them all in the resources section at the back of this book. I encourage you to continue to learn even more. A word of caution: Sometimes we procrastinate in the name of more education. I know I can spend countless hours wanting to learn more and more about a topic, which inevitably makes me think I should go back to school and get a degree in it so I can be an expert! At those times I have to step back and realize that I am just delaying what really must be done.

Step Three: Talk to your advisor

Your advisor should be talking to you about this, but if not, then you have to take the lead. The truth is, if they are not talking to you about it, it is very likely they are not implementing BRI in your portfolio.

Here are some questions for your advisor:

- Have you heard of Biblically Responsible Investing?
- Do you use it in my portfolios?
- Do you know specifically what kind of business practices I am investing in?

If your advisor is not aware of these issues, then you have a great opportunity to start to educate them. Give them a copy of this book or another book listed in the resource section.

To avoid embarrassment, they may make light of

BRI, or tell you that it is not important, but now you know the truth. You will be standing by yourself on Judgment Day, so now is the time to evaluate your own personal beliefs and your responsibility in making a positive change.

Step Four: Screen your current portfolio

Don't be fooled by those who try to excuse these sins, for the anger of God will fall on all those who disobey him. Don't participate in the things these people do.
Ephesians 5:5-7 (NLT)

If you are looking to expose the "worthless deeds of evil and darkness," screening your own portfolio is the only way to do it. No advisor on his own can have enough time or knowledge to know the business practices of each company you own. The same company can have many lines of business, such as selling baby products and abortifacient drugs. To know what you own, your portfolio holdings need to be run through a screening database that will tell you what percentage of your holdings are in violation of the following areas:

- Abortion
- Abortion Philanthropy
- Pornography
- Adult Entertainment
- Alternative Lifestyles

- Alcohol
- Tobacco
- Gambling
- Corporate Governance Issues

Even the money managers managing mutual funds and portfolios in these specialty areas, whether it is Socially Responsible Investing or Biblically Responsible Investing, use this software to stay up-to-date and informed.

If your advisor does not have access to this software, in the resource section you will see where you can send a list of your holdings to be screened.

You *must* find out what business practices you are currently invested in to really understand the power of BRI. This is where most investors get stuck. They say, "If I know, then I'll have to do something about it." Well, yes. That is the point!

Step Five: Demand it

One reason many Christian advisors do not offer BRI is because their clients are not asking for it. You can understand why that might be. Business owners stay in business by providing the products and services their customers demand. That is why I believe this movement of Biblically Responsible Investing really needs to begin with individual investors like you. If Christian clients start demanding BRI, more advisors will offer it and together we can continue to grow God-honoring businesses and defund the others.

Here is a quote from an article entitled "6 Sustainability Investing Trends for 2015":

> *SRI investment growth is driven by popular demand. In the US SIF survey, 80% of 119 US money managers who responded to a question on why they offer SRI products said **it was in response to client demand**. (emphasis added).*[23]

Whether it is in the SRI space or the BRI space, it is client demand that will drive money managers to create new and better funds to serve our needs. If your advisor does not currently offer BRI funds, you can direct him or her to The Christian Investment Forum at http://christianinvestmentforum.org to learn more.

Step Six: Take action

I pondered the direction of my life,
  and I turned to follow your laws.
I will hurry, without delay,
  to obey your commands.
Evil people try to drag me into sin,

---

[23] Maureen Kline, "6 Sustainability Investing Trends for 2015," Inc.com, http://www.inc.com/maureen-kline/6-sustainability-investing-trends-for-2015.html

but I am firmly anchored to your instructions.
Psalm 119:59-61 (NLT)

If you change nothing about the way you are investing, then nothing changes. Pick something you can do in the next three days to start your ball rolling.

Start today to pray about where God would have you invest. Talk to your spouse and your friends about it. Then follow God's guidance as you seek to align your investments with your faith beliefs.

Advisor Action Plan

The topic of Biblically Responsible Investing hits both a stewardship question and a fiduciary responsibility to your clients. You have an amazing opportunity as an advisor to educate and guide your clients in choosing their investments. They are looking to you for direction and trusting that you understand what is important to them when you build their portfolios.

Since you already read the Investor Action Plan, I know you are praying for God to give you direction about implementing BRI in your own practice. After that:

Step One: Ask the question

In each and every client meeting ask the question, "Are there any specific companies or industries you would prefer not to own in your portfolio due to faith or other reasons?" This will start to give you some great insights as to what is important to your clients.

Expect the reply, "I'm not sure what you mean." This gives you an opportunity to explain that because of moral convictions some people choose not to profit from things such as abortion or pornography. Or you can use your own examples. This is a very non-threatening way to learn about what is important to your clients.

Step Two: Get trained

There are many great resources for you to learn more about the Biblical principles of investing and BRI. If you have not done so already, I strongly encourage you to take the following training programs offered by Kingdom Advisors:

- Kingdom Advisor Core Training: The Core Training teaches you to effectively integrate Biblical financial wisdom into client counsel.
  https://kingdomadvisors.com/training/core-training
- Biblically Responsible Investing—Understanding the Heart of God: The goal of Biblically Responsible Investing is investing that seeks to please and glorify God as a vital act of worship. This online course teaches the why, when, how, and where of Biblically Responsible Investing.

Step Three: Find out what is available at your current Registered Investment Advisor or broker/dealer

Next you should find out what funds and money managers can be used at your current place of work. If you work in a large firm, your choices might be more limited. However, most of the big firms are starting to offer some funds on their platform. The more independent you are, the more options you will have. For a great start, visit www.christianinvestmentforum.org for a list of providers.

Step Four: Invest your own portfolio

If you are just not sure how this whole BRI process works, try it first with your own portfolio so you can talk about it more easily with clients.

Step Five: Find a mentor

If you would like some additional help in implementing BRI in your practice, the BRI Community Group from Kingdom Advisors can match you with an advisor who practices in the same type of firm that you do and can give you guidance on a step-by-step process for you to start implementing change in your practice.

Step Six: Do some soul-searching

When I finally understood BRI at its very core, I

decided I would only invest my client's money in this way. Many advisors take a "toe in the water" approach, and start offering it to certain clients, but give their clients a choice in how they want to invest. There is nothing wrong with this approach—you have to start somewhere. I have great admiration for every advisor who is willing to move out of their comfort zone and trust God on this issue.

I decided if I was against these business practices, I could not help clients to invest this way and work against my beliefs. For example, I am adamantly opposed to abortion, and I cannot help clients to fund that industry.

Every advisor starts out at a different place on this journey and takes a different amount of time to implement it. My hope is that you will START SOMEWHERE. Take some action and find out what an amazing blessing BRI can be in your life and in your business.

Do not despise these small beginnings, for the Lord rejoices to see the work begin...

Zechariah 4:10 (NLT)

Resources

The Christian Investment Forum
http://christianinvestmentforum.org
The Christian Investment Forum is an association of Christian investment professionals and companies. They strive to educate financial advisors and the wider public on the benefits of Biblically Responsible Investing through research that leads to credibility, training that leads to knowledge, and networking that leads to influence.

Kingdom Advisors
www.kingdomadvisors.com
Kingdom Advisors' roots were planted in 1997 when Larry Burkett, Co-Founder of Crown Financial Ministries, brought together 16 friends and fellow professionals with a commitment to Biblically wise financial advice to form the Christian Financial Planning Institute (CFPI).
Kingdom Advisors' ongoing desire is to serve its members by helping them offer Biblically wise

financial advice that is rooted in the firm foundation of God's Word and by providing valuable fellowship for like-minded, faithful advisors. The training is designed to equip members with timeless resources and practical tools so that Kingdom Advisors proves to be a trustworthy partner for advisors and a trusted standard within the financial services industry.

Training Programs

Biblically Responsible Investing: Understanding the Heart of God

https://kingdomadvisors.com/training/topical-courses/biblically-responsible-investing

A video-based, self-study course for investment advisors, brokers, and other investment professionals who wish to examine the why and how of applying Biblical principles to the investment selection process. Designed to be helpful to those new to Biblically Responsible Investing and to veterans as well.

Stock and Mutual Fund Screening Tools

For Investors who would like their portfolio screened: Please contact your financial advisor or email info@beaconwealth.com for a complimentary portfolio screening.

BRI Institute

http://briinstitute.com

BRII's mission is to provide Christian investors with the high quality information they need about the activities of public companies so that they can make good stewardship decisions about how to properly invest the money the Lord has entrusted to them. Using Biblical standards, BRII has identified over sixty activities that are of concern to Christians and has built an extensive database that catalogues corporate violations of these Biblical principles.

ENSOGO

http://www.ensogoanalytics.com/products-page/
ENSOGO Analytics offers unique rating analysis and reports of mutual funds and ETFs on their Environmental, Social, and Governance (ESG) and Biblically Responsible Innvesting (BRI) attributes. These reports are generated quickly and easily, and provide comprehensive ESG insights.

eVALUEator

http://evalueator.com
eVALUEator exists to provide the best tools on the market for screening investments according to morally and Biblically Responsible ways. They have sought to stay ahead of the game in three main areas: 1) providing customers with the most up-to-date research, 2) continually improving software to ensure an easy and fast user experience, and 3) maintaining an excellent, personal customer-service experience.

IW Financial

http://info.iwfinancial.com
IW Financial is a leading provider of environmental,

social, and governance (ESG) and faith-based research, consulting, and portfolio management solutions for asset management firms, managed accounts sponsors, institutional investors, plan sponsors, and investment advisors.

The firm's expertise positions clients to benefit from two of the major trends shaping the financial services industry today: demand for issues-based stock screening, and growing interest in highly customized investment portfolios that reflect the values of an institution or an individual.

Books

Kingdom Gains: What Every Christian Should Know Before Investing, Dwight Short

Profits or Principles: Investing Without Compromise, Dwight Short

Investing With Integrity, Loran Graham

Blogs

Faith & Business, Eventide Funds
http://eventidefunds.com/faith-and-business/

True Wealth Spotlight, Beacon Wealth Consultants
http://www.beaconwealth.com/true-wealth-spotlight/

Acknowledgements

In a book about my testimony, of course, I thank God for putting me on this path. It has been one of the biggest challenges, and my greatest blessing, to be put on this journey and to get to share it with others.

I have the greatest admiration for my husband, Rick Laymon, who served as my guide on this journey. He has been implementing BRI solutions for his clients for two decades and has been an amazing role model. He had confidence in God's plan for me long before I did, and I am grateful to be his partner in all things.

There are a number of pioneers as well as current leaders in the field of Biblically Responsible Investing, and each of them has played a unique and important role in my understanding of BRI:

Finny Kuruvilla, Portfolio Manager at Eventide Funds

Dan Hardt, Creator of the *BRI: Understanding the Heart of God* training program

Rusty Leonard, Founder of the BRI Institute

John Siverling, Executive Director, The Christian Investment Forum

Dwight Short, Author of *Kingdom Gains* and *Profits or Principles*

Mike Kuckel, Alex Ellis, and again my husband, Rick, all who are BRI advisors who helped me understand the objections that investors and advisors face when implementing BRI.

I am also blessed to know two men who have fully dedicated their lives to educating business leaders to incorporate biblical values and teaching into their business to make a greater impact for the Kingdom:

Ron Blue, Founder of Kingdom Advisors and the Core Curriculum Training. This is the training that helped me realize that financial advisors can live out their faith at work.

Buck Jacobs, Founder of the C12 Group, who inspired me to share my testimony so that others might find the peace in Christ that I have found.

About the Author

Cassandra Laymon is the President of Beacon Wealth Consultants. She holds a master's degree in Adult Education and an MBA, both from Rutgers University. She is a CERTIFIED FINANCIAL PLANNER™ and a Qualified Kingdom Advisor. She is a dynamic public speaker and has presented at national conferences for the C12 Group and Kingdom Advisors. She currently leads the Biblically Responsible Investing special interest group for financial professionals who are members of Kingdom Advisors.

As a former healthcare executive, she previously managed Education and Organizational Development for a 5,000 employee healthcare system in which her responsibilities included strategic planning, team and leadership development, meeting design and facilitation, and patient satisfaction. These skills, combined with her passion for lifelong learning, have greatly equipped her for her present role leading strategy and developing client education at BWC. Cassie and her husband, Rick (CEO of Beacon Wealth Consultants), married and merged their financial advisory businesses together in 2012. They enjoy collaborating on the business, traveling, theater, cycling, sharing books, and going on adventures with their three children, Sam, Bethany, and Carson.

To book Cassandra at your next event,
or to access the Press Kit for "I Found Jesus in the Stock Market:
How Biblically Responsible Investing Can Change Your Heart, Too!"
please go to:
http://www.IFoundJesusInTheStockMarket.com
or email mailto:info@beaconwealth.com
or call 540-345-3891

47786666R00071

Made in the USA
Middletown, DE
03 September 2017